IMAGES
of England

ASTON AND
PERRY BARR

A view of Aston village, 1868. The Holte almshouses, completed in 1656, are on the left and the graceful spire of Aston church, dedicated to St Peter and Paul, is in the distance.

IMAGES

of England

ASTON AND PERRY BARR

Compiled by
Maria Twist

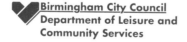

Birmingham City Council
Department of Leisure and
Community Services

TEMPUS

Tempus Publishing Limited
The Mill, Brimscombe Port,
Stroud, Gloucestershire, GL5 2QG

ISBN 0 7524 1808 4

Typesetting and origination by
Tempus Publishing Limited
Printed in Great Britain by
Midway Clark Printing, Wiltshire

The Aston viaduct, *c.* 1837. The Grand Junction Railway passed very close to Aston on its way to join the Manchester to Liverpool line at Warrington, although there was no station there until 1854. The ten-arched viaduct crossed the river Tame twice as it looped around Aston church. Aston Hall can be seen on the left above the trees.

Contents

Acknowledgements

All the photographs, except for three, are from the collections in Birmingham Central Library. Those on pp. 94 and 122 are reproduced by courtesy of the Birmingham Post and Mail Ltd. Those on p. 56 (bottom) and p. 77 were kindly supplied by my husband, Frank Twist, who has given me every possible encouragement. Not only has he kept the home fires burning, but his own knowledge of the area has been invaluable and I am most grateful for his help. I should also like to thank Martin Flynn, Central Library Manager, and my colleagues in the Local Studies and History Service for their help and support.

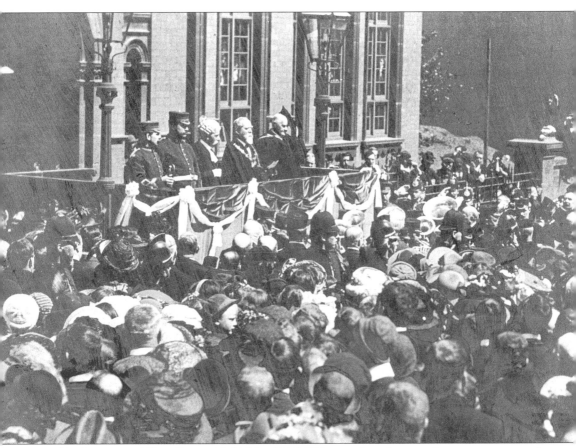

Proclamation of King George V, 11 May 1910. This must have been an important moment for Aston Manor's mayor, Alderman Alfred Taylor. The Borough of Aston Manor was very short-lived, lasting from 1903 until it became part of the City of Birmingham in 1911.

Introduction

Aston is an inner-city suburb of Birmingham, lying some two to three miles north of the city centre and known to many as the home of Aston Villa Football Club. This book aims to show, by means of photographs taken over a period of more than a century, that Aston has a fascinating history in its own right. First recorded in the Domesday Book of 1086 as Estone, it was a large parish in Warwickshire covering 10,000 acres with a mill, a priest and therefore probably a church, woodland and plough land. The area once known as Aston Manor was only one of several manors in the parish and it is this area which falls within the scope of this book. Besides the village of Aston, with its church and manor house of Aston Hall, once the seat of the Holte family, the area includes Lozells and New Town. Aston University, which is Birmingham's second university, lies just outside it. Governed by Aston Manor Local Board from 1869 until it became an Urban District Council in 1890, Aston Manor was incorporated as a borough in 1903 and was finally absorbed into Birmingham in 1911.

Perry Barr is an outer suburb of Birmingham, beyond Aston to the north and north west. Although not as celebrated as Aston, some will know of its connection with the famous Birchfield Harriers athletic club. Also mentioned in the Domesday Book, its name derives from the Old English word for 'pear tree'. It was a hamlet in the Staffordshire parish of Handsworth and is linked to Aston by means of Birchfield, also in Handsworth parish. There is confusion and even disagreement about the boundaries of Perry Barr, possibly caused by naming the station on the Grand Junction Railway Perry Barr when Birchfield would perhaps have been more appropriate. This book concentrates on the area around the church of Perry and the site of Perry Hall, its lost Elizabethan manor house, and includes Birchfield.

Perry Barr was chosen to accompany Aston as it provides an interesting contrast to its near neighbour. By the end of the nineteenth century, Aston was completely developed as an area of mixed residential and industrial use and no trace of its rural past remained. Perry Barr, on the other hand, retained some rural features until relatively recently. Absorbed into Birmingham in 1928 as the lesser of two evils, the greater being incorporation into West Bromwich, Perry Barr's housing estates developed from this period onwards. Gradually the farmland, which grew mainly wheat and potatoes according to Kelly's *Directory of Birmingham* of 1910, was swallowed up by suburbia.

Both Aston and Perry Barr have been industrially important on account of excellent transport links by road, rail and canal. The Birmingham and Fazeley Canal runs northwards on the eastern side of Aston and joins the Tame Valley Canal at Salford Bridge. The Tame Valley Canal runs westwards through Perry Barr so the whole area had access to the country's canal network. The Grand Junction Railway also passed through Aston and Perry Barr and a branch from Aston to Sutton Coldfield and Lichfield was added later. With the building of the Aston Expressway and Spaghetti Junction, the area is at the heart of the country's road system too. The river Tame links both Aston and Perry Barr and was used for water-powered mills in both places. Aston also has water from artesian wells which resulted in a large number of breweries being established there. The HP Sauce factory, founded as the Midland Vinegar Company in 1875, also made use of well water. With the departure of Ansells Brewery after an industrial dispute in 1981, all the old breweries have disappeared, leaving the more recent Aston Manor Brewery as the only one in Birmingham. Other famous firms were Hercules Cycles, George Ellison's Switchgear, Martindale's Crocodile Works in Alma Street, Joseph Harris's dry-cleaning business and the ICI/IMI complex which is partly within Perry Barr.

Aston also has some interesting literary connections. Washington Irving, the American writer, published his *Sketch Book* in 1819/20 and its sequel *Bracebridge Hall* in 1822, both based on life at Aston Hall where he had stayed as a visitor. Sir Arthur Conan Doyle, of Sherlock Holmes fame, worked as an assistant to Dr Hoare at Clifton House, 63 Aston Road North, for a few months each year during the period 1879-82. In more recent times, Walter Allen, one of the Birmingham Group of writers active during the 1930s, was born in Aston and educated at King Edward VI Grammar School, Aston. Reginald Smith, writer and broadcaster and the husband of the novelist Olivia Manning, was educated at the same school.

Throughout this century, Aston and Perry Barr have been subjected to major changes which have rendered them almost unrecognizable. The photographs in the last chapter of the book reflect changes to the main road routes north from the city, caused by increased traffic volume and the need for speedy links to the motorway network. Bridges have been constantly rebuilt, whether over road, railway or canal, and old housing has been torn down and replaced with new houses, flats and maisonettes, some of which have been demolished in their turn. These events were meticulously recorded and often resulted in interesting and even artistic images. The impression remains, however, that Aston and Perry Barr have both been by-passed in the rush to be somewhere else and that a great deal of their past has been sacrificed in the process.

The village of Aston. This pastoral scene shows Aston before the building of the Grand Junction Railway in 1837.

One
Scenes in Aston

Aston village, 1897. By this time Aston had become a densely populated, built-up area. These houses were superior residences with their small front gardens and elegant railings.

Lothersdale, 1897. This and the adjoining house in Aston village was the home of Sir John Benjamin Stone until 1877. Many of the photographs in this book are from the Stone collection. Stone was born in Aston in 1838 and became a renowned photographer, the first mayor of Sutton Coldfield in 1886 and MP for East Birmingham in 1895.

The garden front of Lothersdale. On the left stands a mulberry tree. Lothersdale was the name of the village in Yorkshire from which Sir J.B. Stone's wife came. The Stone family later moved to the Grange in Erdington.

The garden of Mr Knight's house in Sutton Street, Aston, 1869. This was Bay Tree Villa, the home of Frederick Knight Jnr, of Smith, Stone and Knight's Union Paper Mills in Lander Street. Sir J.B. Stone's business interests made him wealthy enough to spend time on foreign travel and photography.

Holte almshouses in Aston Lane, 1897. The almshouses were demolished in 1929 in spite of protests by the Birmingham Civic Society, which had suggested a programme of renovation instead.

Aston village from the Aston Tavern, 7 June 1926. This tavern is in Aston Lane, now Aston Hall Road, near to the church and the Serpentine Grounds where the annual Onion Fair was held until 1969. Although still standing, the tavern is now completely derelict.

Aston Vicarage, 21 June 1967. This fine Georgian house was demolished soon afterwards to make way for the Aston Expressway.

The house of Mr Frederick Roberts, Aston parish clerk, 1874. The stone pillar on the left was removed by Mr Roberts from its former position as one of two which stood at the end of the Chestnut Avenue leading to Aston Hall.

Mr Frederick Roberts and Mrs Roberts in their garden adjoining the vicarage, 1874.

Six Ways, Aston, showing St Paul's church, Lozells, in the 1880s. J.A. Chatwin was the architect of this church, which was built in 1880. Thomas Riches & Son was a grocer's with several branches in the area. The post office is next door.

Six Ways, Aston, in the 1880s. Six Ways was formed when Victoria Road was made in the late 1850s, providing a link between the Birmingham to Lichfield and Birmingham to Walsall turnpike roads.

14

Six Ways, Aston, looking down Victoria Road, *c.* 1900. Tramlines are being laid in the foreground. On the left of the lamp post is Thomas Osborn's coffee house and opposite is the new National Provincial Bank.

Aston Cross. This view shows the old clock which was erected in 1854 and replaced with a new one in 1891. The design was apparently intended to echo the architecture of Aston Hall. A steam tram is making its way along Lichfield Road towards Erdington, while behind the clock some cabs are waiting for fares.

The present Aston Cross clock, c. 1906. On the left is a cabmen's shelter and in the background is the Midland Bank, Aston Cross library and the Golden Cross Inn, now renamed O'Reilly's.

Aston Cross, c. 1914. Electric trams are now running along Lichfield Road and Park Road. Since Ansells Brewery closed after a union dispute in 1981, a number of car showrooms have opened, completely altering the area's character.

Aston Cross, looking towards the city centre, 29 June 1973. The clock has since been moved to the centre of a new roundabout a few yards away.

A street scene in Aston, 1898. At least two of the boys have no shoes, indicating the poverty that existed in parts of Aston.

Old houses in Victoria Road, c. 1900. This shows part of the area once known as The City.

Two
Aston Hall and Park

The east front of Aston Hall, 28 August 1890. Built by Sir Thomas Holte during the period 1618 to 1635, probably to designs by John Thorpe, Aston Hall is a magnificent Jacobean manor house set in the midst of an inner-city suburb.

View of Aston Hall, 1868. In 1818, Aston Hall was sold and let to James Watt Jnr, the son of James Watt the engineer. He made his home there until his death in 1848. On the left is the glass pavilion designed by J.J. Bateman in 1858 and used as a museum and art gallery, which has now been demolished.

Long Gallery at Aston Hall, *c.* 1890. The Long Gallery with its panelling and beautiful moulded plaster ceiling is one of the glories of Aston Hall.

The kitchen at Aston Hall, *c.* 1890. The spits in front of the open hearth were turned by a smoke jack in the chimney which still survives.

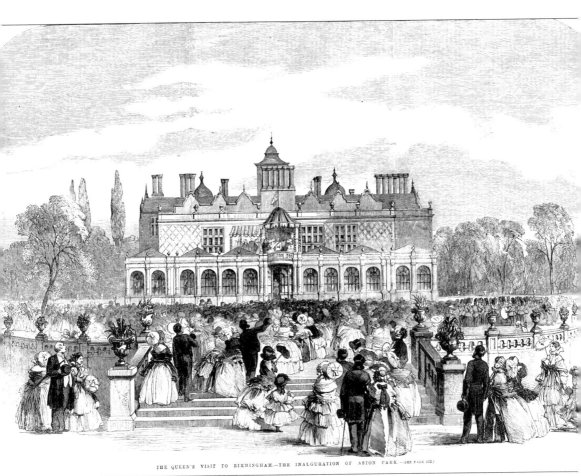

THE QUEEN'S VISIT TO BIRMINGHAM.—THE INAUGURATION OF ASTON PARK.—[SEE PAGE 22.]

Queen Victoria's visit to Aston Hall, 1858. This print appeared in the *Illustrated London News*. In 1858, Aston Hall was purchased by the Aston Hall and Park Company. Queen Victoria was invited to perform the opening ceremony, one of only two visits she made to Birmingham as Queen. This early attempt to transform Aston Hall and Park into a place of public entertainment failed and it was eventually acquired by Birmingham Corporation in 1864. Aston Hall became the first 'country' house to be opened to the public by a local authority.

Aston Hall from the leads over the Long Gallery, c. 1890.

Garret, Aston Hall. This undated photograph shows the garret which used to be referred to as Dick's Garret, thought to be haunted. The reason for the name seems to have been forgotten.

Aston Hall, 1897. This view shows a secret cupboard behind a hinged chair under the staircase, complete with skeleton! The great oak staircase still bears the scars of its bombardment by Parliamentarian forces during the Civil War siege of 1643.

Aston Hall. An attractive range of eighteenth-century outbuildings is shown here in a modern photograph.

Donkeys for hire at the corner of Aston Park opposite the church, 1874.

The Great Hall at Aston Hall in January 1974.

Entrance gate to Aston Hall and Park, 1874. The gate and lodges were built in the Gothic style by Sir Lister Holte between 1754 and 1757. They were demolished in 1959 when the road was widened. The stalls on the left are possibly selling refreshments while on the right donkeys wait patiently to be hired.

Aston Park. This postcard was sent from Aston Vicarage on 30 March 1905. In the time of Sir Thomas Holte, Aston Park contained over 300 acres of woods, pasture, arable land, orchards, gardens and fishponds, and a herd of deer. In the nineteenth century the estate was gradually sold off for building and is now only one-sixth of its former size.

Old oak trees in Aston Park. These oaks were obviously nearing the end of their lives when this postcard view was taken, probably in the early years of the twentieth century.

Parks inspection, 1926. The City Council Parks Committee are admiring the box bed in front of Aston Hall, with the fine fleet of chauffeur driven vehicles in which they have arrived neatly parked to one side. The gardens of Aston Hall were being re-designed at this period. The planning was done by the Birmingham Civic Society, which also designed and donated the stone terrace and steps in front of the Hall.

Inauguration of the new fountain at Aston Park, 1934. The sculptor William Bloye was commissioned to undertake this work, which was part of the on-going redevelopment of the Park. The fountain is still there although no longer functioning as a fountain.

Aston Park was the venue for the Pageant of Birmingham in July 1938, held to commemorate the granting of the Charter of Incorporation to Birmingham in 1838. This picture shows the re-enactment of the Battle of Crécy.

These performers are being directed off the set after their episode is finished.

Archers performing in the Battle of Crécy.

The pageant culminated in a final procession of all the performers.

Three
Aston Streets

Courtyard in Aston, 1898. In Aston and other inner-city areas many dwellings were built round courtyards, or courts as they were usually called, at the back of the row of houses fronting the street itself. The doorway on the left of the picture led through the entry to the street. Some of the houses were therefore 'back-to-backs', which were condemned as unhealthy, although many were inhabited until relatively recently.

A courtyard in Aston, 1898. The toddler on the left is standing on what looks like a child's wooden high chair.

Courtyard in Aston, c. 1898. The birdcage hanging on the wall probably held a canary. Courts were often brightened up with pots of flowers on the window sills.

Street scene in Aston, *c.* 1898. Houses built in the earlier part of the nineteenth century were sometimes of three storeys but may have been only one room deep.

Street scene in Aston, 1898. The building in the centre has been strengthened with iron braces. The advertisements are interesting historically but hardly improve the appearance of the street.

Aston Road opposite Pritchett Street, *c.* 1914. The three-storey house with shops on the street frontage has a terrace of houses built at the back. This was an improvement on the enclosed courts.

New Town Row looking towards Cecil Street, *c.* 1914. The New Town area of Aston started to develop in the early nineteenth century and became a shopping centre with its own High Street between New Town Row and Six Ways, Aston.

New Town Row showing the corner of Hatchett Street, *c.* 1914. The girl on the right has stopped in the road to look at the photographer with no fear of being run over.

A scene in New Town between the wars. The man smoking a pipe is wearing a bowler hat and white scarf which was a popular style of dress at the time.

The railway bridge in Aston Lane, *c.* 1933. Gas lamps were still widely used for street lighting at this period.

Junction of Aston Road North and Avenue Road, 19 June 1937. This picture shows a mix of factories, shops and houses which was typical of the area. On the left is an early Belisha beacon marking the pedestrian crossing. These were introduced in the 1930s and were named after Leslie Hore-Belisha, who was Minister of Transport at the time.

Summer Lane, *c.* 1949. On the right is a Birmingham City Council bus-stop sign familiar to all but the youngest Brummies.

Gee Street, New Town, *c.* 1952. The girl is wearing a box-pleated gymslip which was standard school uniform. The younger boys are wearing short trousers as they did all the year round until they were about thirteen or fourteen.

Numbers 37-39 New John Street West, 30 November 1956. This area has now been completely redeveloped as much of Aston has been in recent years.

A court adjoining 58 New John Street West. Toilets and wash-houses, or brewhouses as they were called, were usually outside and were communal.

Asylum Road, 1960.

Alma Street, November 1960. The shops on the right are boarded up prior to demolition.

Numbers 138-142 Church Street, Lozells, January 1981. Some older houses were refurbished under the City's Urban Renewal Scheme instead of being swept away and replaced with new housing.

Numbers 55, 56 and 57 Barker Street, Lozells, April 1981. The development of this street began in the late 1830s and the houses were mainly occupied by craftsmen from the Jewellery Quarter of Birmingham, clerks and commercial travellers. These houses date from about 1840 and are now listed buildings.

Four
Churches and Chapels

Aston Old church. This early postcard view shows the bend in the river Tame which no longer exists. A straighter course was engineered alongside the railway line and the old loop gradually silted up.

Aston Old church, *c.* 1870. Although a medieval church replaced an earlier church on this site, all that remains is the fifteenth century tower and the spire, which was partly rebuilt in 1776/77.

Aston church before restoration. The body of the church was rebuilt by J.A. Chatwin between 1879 and 1890, so this photograph must antedate this work.

A monument to William Holte, who died in 1514, and his wife Joanna in the north aisle of Aston church, 1910.

St John's church, Perry Barr. The church was built in 1831/32 and paid for by John Gough of Perry Hall. Before this time, people in Perry Barr had to go to church at St Mary's, Handsworth. Cows in the field by the church show the rural nature of Perry Barr which was in contrast to the densely populated areas of Aston and Birchfield.

St John's church, Perry Barr, from the Zig-Zag Bridge.

St Silas' church, Lozells. This church, consecrated in 1854 and designed by F.W. Fiddian, is now a listed building. Many new churches were built in Aston as the population grew.

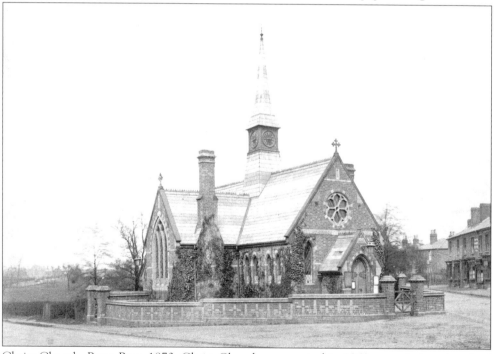

Christ Church, Perry Barr, 1873. Christ Church was erected in 1862 as a mission church of St John's and was licensed until 1926. It has now been demolished after having been used by a timber merchant for a number of years.

The interior of St Mary's, Aston
Brook. Built in 1863 and designed by
J. Murray, this handsome church was
demolished in 1971.

St Mary's, Aston Brook, c. 1952. The
tower was added in 1882.

St Matthias' church. Situated on the corner of Farm Street and Wheeler Street, Lozells, this church was designed by J.L. Pedley and consecrated in 1855. In 1948 it was closed and subsequently demolished.

Postcard view of Lozells Street Hall. This was a Methodist chapel designed by Joseph Crouch and Edmund Butler in 1893. The hall was famous for its orchestra, which was under the leadership of John Frederick Yoxall for many years. His brother Henry Yoxall had been instrumental in founding the mission.

Aston Villa Wesleyan Chapel. In around 1872 the members of the Sunday school cricket team formed a football club which came to be known as Aston Villa Football Club. The chapel is now a Pentecostal church.

Congregational chapel, Park Road, Aston. Opened in 1874, this chapel was demolished in the 1950s.

Six Ways Baptist church, Aston. This church was built in the early 1860s and is still standing, having listed building status.

Guildford Street Baptist chapel. A hall originally built by A.J. Abbott, this building was taken under the charge of Six Ways Baptist church in 1867. The whole area has now been redeveloped.

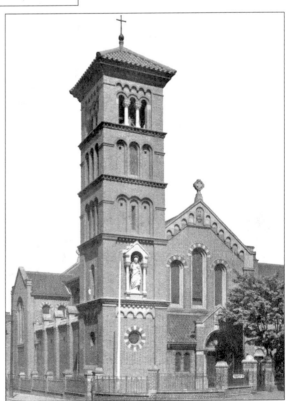

The Roman Catholic church of the Sacred Heart, Witton Road, 1935. This church was designed in the Italian Romanesque style by G.B. Cox and consecrated in 1933.

Five
Public Buildings and Schools

Aston Manor Council House and Library. Designed by William Henman, the building was officially opened on 5 January 1882. This photograph was probably taken at about this time and shows two horse-drawn fire engines. Aston Library still occupies the building. About 1883, the librarian, Robert K. Dent, inaugurated a series of free lectures for the public which were a great success and were an early example of library extension activities.

Aston Library reference section, 1913.

Aston Library delivery counter, 1913. The closed access system in use at this time is clearly shown here. An indicator board informed borrowers whether a book was in or out.

Aston Cross Library, 1913. This was one of the libraries erected at the expense of the philanthropist Andrew Carnegie all over the country and known as Carnegie Libraries. The library opened on 30 October 1903 on a site given by William and Edward Ansell. Unfortunately it fell victim to local authority cuts and closed in the 1990s.

Birchfield Library, 1913. The building was opened in 1874 as Perry Barr Institute and in 1886 was taken over as a public library, a function which it still has today.

Cottage Baths, Brearley Street, October 1950. Opened on 19 February 1912, these baths were erected by the Baths Committee to provide people with washing facilities in areas of dense population where many houses did not have bathrooms.

Victoria Road, Aston, *c.* 1900. Victoria Road Baths can be seen on the left. Erected by Aston Local Board, the baths were opened on 5 October 1892. During the winter a floor was laid over the first-class swimming bath and gymnastic classes and other activities were held.

The old police station, Perry Barr, 1906. This building was demolished in the early 1950s for road widening.

Lozells Street Primary School, 9 September 1974. This school was opened by Aston School Board in 1882. The first kitchen for cookery classes under Aston School Board opened here in 1886. It has now been rebuilt on a site between Wheeler Street and Clifford Street.

A class at Lozells Street Primary School, c. 1924. The pupils are apparently having a lesson in cutting and folding paper. Not many schools today would have a Union Jack standing in the corner!

Aston Hall Junior and Infants' School, 11 September 1972. This was opened in 1886 as Aston Lane Board School. The name was changed in 1935 and the school closed in 1972.

St Matthias' School, Wheeler Street, 6 March 1967. St Matthias' National School was opened in 1858. It has now been demolished.

Anglesey Infants' School, September 1972. This school was opened in 1894 as Anglesey Street Board School. A new school in Church Street has now been built.

Anglesey Infants' School, September 1972.

St Silas' Church of England Primary School, Church Street, Lozells, 10 July 1973. A National School was established here in 1852. The school closed in 1973.

Alma Street School. This school was opened in 1878 as Alma Street Board School and closed in 1969.

Aston Manor Technical School, Whitehead Road, in the early 1900s. The school was founded in 1891 as the result of the passing of the Technical Education Act in 1889. Later it became Aston Technical College and it is now the Aston annexe of Handsworth College of Further Education.

An art class at Aston Technical School in the early 1900s.

Six
Shops and Factories

Harry Juggins and family resplendent in their Ford Model T motor car outside his father's shop at 8 Lozells Road, c. 1910. Alfred Juggins was official photographer to the Aston Theatre Royal and many stage celebrities visited his studio, among them the Fred Karno troupe when Charlie Chaplin was a member. Harry founded Birmingham Commercial Films Ltd in 1938.

Harry Wilks & Co., cutlers and glass warehouse operators in New Town Row, Aston, 1898.

Herbert Millington's butchers shop at 2 Potter's Hill, Aston, in the 1920s.

A. Barnes' bakers shop, Potter's Hill, *c.* 1920. This photograph was taken by Alfred Juggins of Lozells Road.

E. Wallin, building contractors and timber merchants, of 16 Upper Webster Street, Aston, in the 1920s.

Henry Poolton, a greengrocer in Lichfield Road, *c.* 1935.

Thompson's greengrocers at the junction of Aston Road North and Sutton Street, *c.* 1935.

Aston Station Stores, Lichfield Road, 2 March 1954.

Tom Hartley's betting shop, Aston Road, *c.* 1960.

A.V. Spilsbury & Co., boot and shoe dealers, 262-264 New Town Row, in the 1950s.

Transport Café at 380 Lichfield Road, Aston, 9 July 1965.

Workmen at E.C. Bellamy & Co., lamp-makers, of 129 Pritchett Street, Aston, c. 1900.

Aston Flint Glass Works belonging to B. & W. Gibbins, Bagot Street, Aston. This engraving, and the one below, appeared in Wrightson's *New Triennial Directory of Birmingham* of 1818.

Aston Flint Glass Works, Bagot Street. The proprietors' rather fine house faced the street, while the works had access to the canal at the rear.

Old malt factory, Johnstone Street, Perry Barr, 21 June 1966.

Disused malthouse, Johnstone Street, 21 June 1966.

Reuben Heaton & Co., fishing reel makers, 38-40 New Street, Aston, 1916.

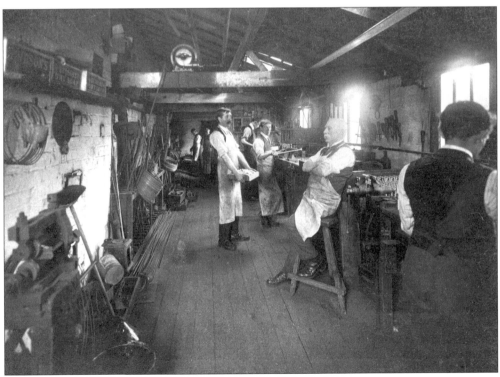

Workers at Reuben Heaton & Co., 1916.

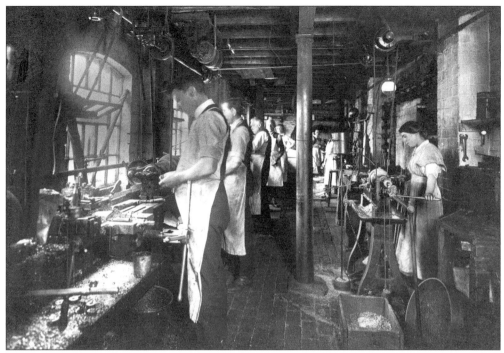

Workers, including a woman machine operator, at Reuben Heaton & Co., 1916. Although women had always worked in Birmingham's workshops, the First World War allowed many more women to enter employment as men's labour was in short supply.

Workers at Reuben Heaton & Co., 1916.

Dunlop's Manor Mills in Rocky Lane, Aston, *c.* 1920.

Boat-building and repair workshop at Perry Park, 12 March 1952.

An aerial view of Cheston Road, Aston, 1926.

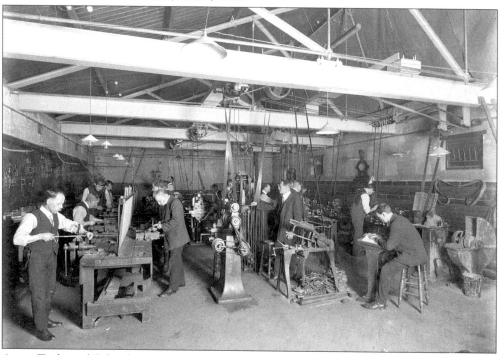

Aston Technical School munitions classes, 1915/16.

An Ansells Brewery dray, 1951. Breweries, dairies, bakeries and coal merchants were among the last businesses to use horses for transport. On May Day, these horses would have been gaily decorated with flowers and ribbons.

At the back of 82 Villa Street, Lozells, 7 July 1919. The small workshops of ETP Co. Ltd, pressworkers, and the Reliance Pattern Making Co. show the diversity of local industry even in such relatively recent times.

Seven
Sport and Leisure

Barnum and Bailey's Circus, Lichfield Road, Aston, c. 1900.

Aston Villa Ground showing Witton Stand, 1900-1905. Standing from the left, no. 6 may be Mr Dunkley, no. 7 is Joshua Margoschis, no. 8 is Jack Urry, a regular contributor to *Villa News and Record*, no. 9 may be Charles Johnstone, no. 10 Isaac Whitehouse, no. 14 William Cooke and no. 19 Jimmy Lees (manager of the Holte Hotel and a director of Aston Villa). Seated from left, no. 2 is Dr Vincent Jones, no. 3 George Ramsey, no. 4 Frederick Rinder (Aston Villa Chairman), no. 5 Joseph Ansell (Aston Villa President), no. 7 may be Mr Vickerstaffe and no. 8 Mr P. Bate. Unfortunately the occasion depicted here is unknown but may have been a charity sports event.

Sam Durban, Captain of Aston Unity
Cricket Club, c. 1900. The club was
founded in 1868 by W. Hundy and
Tom and Joe Woodward. From 1876
to 1884 matches were played on a
ground in Aston Lane; later, under the
leadership of Sam, Edward and Charles
Durban, a ground was leased in
Trinity Road. The club now has a
ground at Coppice Lane, Bassetts
Pole.

A group of Birchfield Harriers at the Alexander Stadium, Perry Barr, seen a few years after the
Second World War at an informal Sunday afternoon training session. The champion woman
athlete Gladys Lunn, known as Sally, is sitting on the ground in the centre. Birchfield Harriers
was founded in 1877. The Alexander Sports Ground and Stadium was opened on 27 July 1929.
The club now has a new stadium in Perry Park and the old one is in use as a greyhound racing
track.

Aston Lower Grounds showing the gardens and pool. This part of Aston Park, not purchased by Birmingham Council in 1864, was re-opened in 1873 by Henry Quilter, manager of the Holte Hotel, as a place of entertainment called Aston Lower Grounds.

Aston Lower Grounds, c. 1885: a view of the ornamental garden and menagerie. In 1879 a very large building had been erected, housing the Holte Theatre, an art gallery, menagerie, aquarium and restaurants. The venture failed in the 1890s and the Grounds were taken over by Aston Villa Football Club in 1897. All traces of the old building have now disappeared.

Aston Lower Grounds, 1885. The Great Open Air Picture *The War in the Sudan* is an example of the spectacular tableaux which were staged here.

The grandstand for the Open Air Picture in Aston Lower Grounds, 1885.

Aston Hippodrome during demolition, 1980. The Hippodrome opened on 7 December 1908 and closed on 4 June 1960, subsequently being used as a bingo hall. Variety shows, revues and touring pantomimes were staged here. Aston also had the Aston Theatre Royal opened in 1893. In 1927 it became the Astoria Cinema, which closed in 1955. ATV's Alpha Studios occupied the building until 1970 when it was demolished.

Birchfield Cinema, Perry Barr, 18 December 1959. This cinema opened in 1913 and closed on 3 March 1962. The Odeon Cinema in Birchfield Road was the first one in the chain founded by Oscar Deutsch and is now a bingo hall.

The Barton's Arms, Aston, July 1981. Designed by Mr Brassington of James and Lister Lea, The Barton's Arms was built between 1899 and 1901 and is now a listed building. The interior is richly decorated with tiles and stained glass.

Church Tavern, Lichfield Road, Aston, 13 May 1975. This tavern was designed by C.H. Collett and built for the Holte Brewery Company in 1900/01. Although a listed building, it is now derelict.

The Cross Guns on the corner of Frankfort Street, 23 June 1968.

The British Lion, New Town Row, 23 July 1959.

Dewdrop Stores, Alma Street, 25 November 1960.

Boar's Head Inn, Perry Barr, 1893. The name of this inn derives from the heraldic crest of the Gough family of Perry Hall. Next to it was a pound for enclosing stray animals until collected by their owners. Both the old inn and the pound have now disappeared.

Another view of the Boar's Head Inn, 1906.

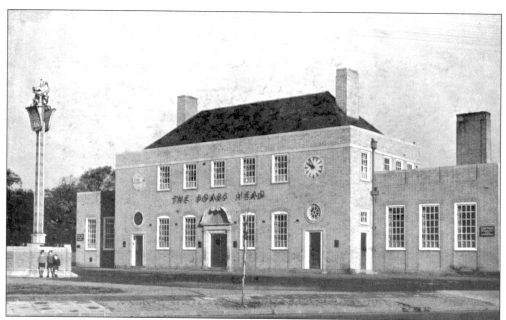

The new Boar's Head Inn, 1937.

The Beeches, Perry Barr, c. 1950. This public house was built to cater for people from a new housing estate built in the 1930s.

Burbury Street Recreation Ground, Aston, 16 April 1956. The land for the recreation ground was presented by William Middlemore, father of John Middlemore, the founder of the Middlemore Children's Emigration Homes. The official opening was on 1 December 1877. Recently it has been claimed that this was the earliest purpose-built children's playground in the country.

The Birmingham Show at Perry Park, 4 September 1970. The Birmingham Show, often called the Flower Show, was held in Handsworth Park until 1969. 1970 was the first year in which it was held at Perry Park.

The Birmingham Show at Perry Park, 4 September 1970.

An attractive thatched shelter at Salford Park, 1925.

Children of the Tree-Lovers' League helping to plant trees at Salford Stadium, 23 April 1970.

Eight
Perry Hall

Perry Hall, 1907. The gentleman in the carriage is Lt-Gen. Sir Somerset Gough-Calthorpe. Perry Hall was built by Sir William Stamford and completed about 1569. In 1669 the estate was purchased by Sir Henry Gough. The Goughs were later linked by marriage to the Calthorpe family of Edgbaston. After Sir Somerset's death in 1912, the hall was left empty and was sold to Birmingham Corporation. As they could not afford to maintain Perry Hall as well as Aston Hall, the former was demolished in 1928.

Perry Hall showing the moat. The moat had been excavated at about the same time as the building of the hall.

Perry Hall showing the covered bridge over the moat. The bridge was a later addition to the building, designed by S.S. Teulon.

The south-west angle of Perry Hall, 1898.

An old notice relating to man traps preserved at Perry Hall, 1906.

Lady Somerset Gough-Calthorpe,
7 October 1907.

Old farm buildings near Perry Hall on the river Tame, 1899. This was Perry Mill Farm which was replaced by a larger building and renamed Home Farm at about this time.

River Tame near Perry Hall.

Perry Hall moat as a children's paddle-boat pool with new bridge, 11 July 1932. The Perry Hall estate was opened by Birmingham Corporation as Perry Hall Playing Fields. Perry Avenue and Cliveden Avenue mark the two drives which led to Perry Hall.

Perry Hall Playing Fields. The paddle-boat pool in use, 14 April 1953.

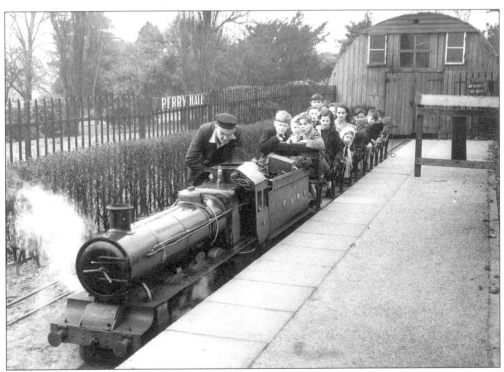

Perry Hall Playing Fields miniature railway, 14 April 1953. Mr Albert Reeve checks on the instruments before his model 4-6-2 Pacific engine, *Mighty Atom*, sets out on another run.

Nine
Scenes in Perry Barr

Perry Barr village, 1900.

Old cottages near St John's church, Perry Barr, *c.* 1906.

The fire brigade at Perry Barr, 1899. In July 1899 a National Fire Brigades' Union camp was held on the Perry Hall estate. Brigades from other parts of the country and from abroad exhibited the latest fire-fighting equipment.

The Zig-Zag Bridge, 1897. Scheduled as an ancient monument, the Zig-Zag Bridge was either erected or refurbished in 1711 to replace an older packhorse bridge carrying the road over the river Tame. Interestingly, the original caption to this photograph calls it Perry or Vandyke Bridge. The zig-zags are V-shaped recesses intended as refuges for pedestrians.

A postcard view of the Zig-Zag Bridge.

Perry Pont House, Perry Barr, 1909. This was a Georgian house situated very close to the Zig-Zag Bridge. When it was sold on 17 March 1932, it was said to have been built on the site of a former Jacobean house, parts of which were still in existence at that time. The house was demolished in 1938.

Entrance to an underground passage at Perry Pont House, 1909. The entrance was made of broken bottle pieces. There were other curiosities in the garden, including a tiny sanctuary, a summer house and statuary. In 1856, the resident was Mr W.H. Osborn, a wine merchant, who was said to have a perfectly green rose in flower in his new rose house. The rose, called *Rosa verdiflora*, was obtained from a French nurseryman.

A stool at Perry Pont House, 1909. An inscription on the stool states that it was part of the root of the tree in which King Charles II sheltered after the battle of Worcester in 1651.

Floodgate at Loke's Farm on the River Tame, c. 1897. This was Perry Mill Farm (see p. 92), occupied by James Loke in the 1870s. The mill was in operation until about this time.

Oldford Farm near Perry Bridge, 1909. This farm was on the opposite side of the Aldridge Road from Perry Mill Farm.

An early postcard view of Perry Barr, showing Birchfield Road.

Wellhead Farm, Aldridge Road, 31 March 1973.

Aldridge Road and Wellhead Lane, March 1928.

Aldridge Road, 3 April 1928.

Wellhead Lane, 25 July 1939. On the left is one of the entrances to Kynoch's works. This ammunition factory became part of the ICI group.

Another view of Wellhead Lane, 25 July 1939. George Ellison's on the right was another well-known local factory which made switch gear.

Walsall Road looking south, March 1947. After the heavy snow of 1947, one of the severest winters of this century, the road was flooded when the thaw eventually arrived.

An old yew tree in Rocky Lane, Perry Barr, 1896. Passing traffic had created a deep hollow way in Rocky Lane of which there is little evidence in the modern road.

A view in Rocky Lane, Perry Barr about 200 yards from the top, 1895.

Rocky Lane, Perry Barr, 1895. One of
Mr Edward Arm's milk floats is just
coming down the lane.

The old manor house in Rocky Lane,
1909. When Perry Hall was built, the
old Manor House was used as a bailiff's
house. It was probably demolished soon
after this photograph was taken. The
finger post points to Perry Barr and
Birmingham to the left and West
Bromwich to the right.

Booth's Farm, Perry Barr, 1900. Booth's Farm was the home for a short while of William Booth, the notorious forger of banknotes and coins. He was eventually captured, tried and found guilty at Stafford Assizes in August 1812 and was one of the last people in England to be hanged for an offence other than murder.

Booth's Farm, Perry Barr, 1903.

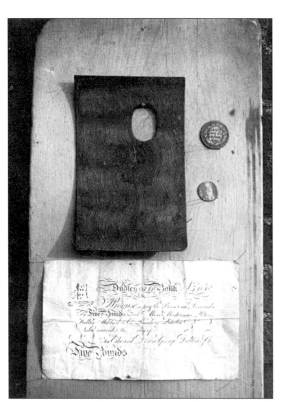

Metal plate, forged note and false coins found in the grounds of Booth's Farm.

Mr Foden and family at Booth's Farm, 1900.

Farm labourers at Booth's Farm, 1900. Booth's Farm was one of the last farms in Perry Barr; it was demolished as recently as 1974. For many years it had stood in a derelict state in the middle of a housing estate.

Herbert Bellamy picking fruit in the garden of the family's house in Wellington Road, Perry Barr, c. 1900. This photograph, together with those on page 67, 110 and 111 are from a collection of glass negatives which were found in a derelict house in Aston. The house in Wellington Road is now part of St Theresa's Roman Catholic church buildings.

Rickyard and farm in Rocky Lane, Perry Barr, 1901.

Edie and Gert Bellamy, c. 1900.

A wintry day in Wellington Road, Perry Barr, *c*. 1900.

College Road, Perry Barr, 2 March 1927.

College Road, Perry Barr, 1929. The road was being widened at about this time and new housing estates built.

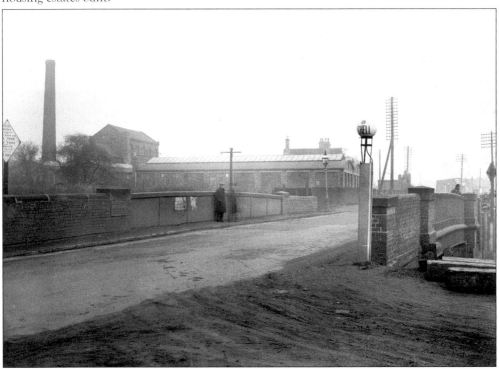

College Road, Perry Barr, 1931. The bridge takes the road over the Tame Valley Canal, which was completed in 1844, much later than most canals in the area.

View of College Road after completion of new houses. After Perry Barr joined Birmingham in 1928, spare land was quickly used for new housing estates which were badly needed for Birmingham's growing population.

Restoration work on the anti-aircraft gun site, Perry Park, 14 February 1958. Many of Birmingham's parks and open spaces were utilized during the Second World War for army camps, anti-aircraft guns or for growing food. Photographs of such installations are few and far between.

Restoration work on the anti-aircraft gun site, Perry Park, 14 February 1958.

Ten
Changing Times

RECONSTRUCTION OF ASTON BRIDGE SUNDAY MARCH 2

A Great Engineering Feat.

This Bridge, weighing **300 tons**, was placed in position in **15½ minutes.**

Reconstruction of Aston Bridge, Sunday 25 March 1906. This bridge carrying the railway over Lichfield Road weighed 300 tons and was said to have been placed in position in 15½ minutes. It was recently replaced again to accommodate the new dual carriageway.

Reconstruction of Aston Lane railway bridge, 1 May 1932.

Aston Lane railway bridge on completion, 28 June 1932.

Lichfield Road, Aston, 1921. This shows the dual carriageway on this section of Lichfield Road under construction, with horse-drawn carts in use.

Lichfield Road, Aston, October 1930. The dual carriageway has been completed. The widening of Lichfield Road to take the increasing volume of traffic meant that a new Salford Bridge spanning the river Tame and the Tame Valley Canal had to be built. This was done using a Government grant for the relief of the unemployed and was officially opened on 13 October 1926.

Salford Bridge, September 1922. This view of the old Salford Bridge was taken just before it was demolished.

Salford temporary bridge, 11 June 1923. A temporary timber bridge was constructed for use while the new stone bridge was being built.

Salford canal bridge, 7 October 1924.

Salford canal bridge, 30 April 1926.

Aldridge Road bridge, Perry Barr, 1932. The Zig-Zag Bridge can be seen to the left of the new road bridge. From this date, only pedestrians were permitted to use the old bridge.

Blakelands Estate, off Aldridge Road, 20 September 1934.

College Road canal bridge, 22 May 1933.

High Street, Aston New Town, 29 August 1953. The bed of Aston Brook, long culverted, has been revealed during repair work.

Salford Flats beside Salford Park, Aston, *c.* 1960. These attractive municipal flats were designed by the City Architect of Birmingham, A.G. Sheppard Fidler, and were built of load-bearing brickwork during a period of steel shortage.

The New Town Redevelopment Area, 14 September 1964. These are sixteen-storey flats and four-storey maisonettes in Unett Street.

Perry Barr Expressway, 14 March 1967. This shows the carriageway looking towards the bus layby south of Whitehead Road. The building of this route and of Aston Expressway has effectively divided Aston into three parts and made it a place to pass through and over without seeing.

A section of Perry Barr Expressway at Aston New Town, 18 January 1967. The construction of a subway to the New Town Shopping Centre is in progress. In the background is the Barton's Arms public house and to the right Aston Hippodrome.

Birchfield flyover, 1 July 1970. On the right is Holy Trinity church, Birchfield.

Perry Barr Shopping Precinct, 1960s. This has already been demolished and replaced by an indoor mall called the One-Stop Shopping Centre, opened in August 1990.

An aerial view of the Birchfield Road underpass. Completed in 1962, this was one of the first underpasses in the country.

Aston Expressway under construction, 31 January 1969. On the right is Aston parish church, lying too close for comfort to the expressway which now carries heavy traffic to and from Birmingham and the motorway network at Spaghetti Junction, cutting a broad swathe through Aston on its way.

The completed Aston Expressway, looking towards Aston parish church, summer 1972.

The official opening of Aston Expressway, 1 May 1972. The ceremony was performed by Councillor Harold Edwards, Chairman of the Public Works Committee. Spaghetti Junction was opened a few weeks later on 24 May 1972 by the Rt Hon. Peter Walker, Minister of the Environment.

An aerial view of Aston Expressway, May 1972. On the right foreground is the corner of a building now part of the University of Central England. In the centre is Dartmouth Circus with its Boulton and Watt beam engine. The spire of Aston church can be seen faintly in the distance, one of the few landmarks still surviving in this area which has seen so much change.